SCIENCE SPOTLIGHT

CRIME-FIGHTING

SCIENCE SPOTLIGHT

CRIME-FIGHTING

IAN GRAHAM

RSVP

RAINTREE
STECK-VAUGHN
PUBLISHERS
The Steck-Vaughn Company

Austin, Texas

Published by Raintree Steck-Vaughn Publishers, an imprint of Steck-Vaughn Company.

Editors: Su Swallow and Shirley Shalit
Designer: Neil Sayer
Production: Peter Thompson
Electronic Production : Scott Melcer
Illustrations: Hardlines, Charlbury Graeme Chambers
Consultant: Peter de Forest, John Jay School of Criminal Justice

The author and publishers would like to thank Anne Holdsworth of The Forensic Science Society for her help in the preparation of this book.

Library of Congress Cataloging-in-Publication Data
Graham, Ian, 1953-
    Crime-fighting / Ian Graham.
        p.   cm. — (Science spotlight)
    Includes index.
    ISBN 0-8114-3840-6
    1. Criminal investigation — Juvenile literature.
    [1. Criminal investigation.] I. Title. II. Series.
    HV8073.8.G73   1995
    363.2'58—dc20   94-13839
                            CIP   AC

Printed in Hong Kong
Bound in the United States
1 2 3 4 5 6 7 8 9 0 99 98 97 96 95 94

ACKNOWLEDGMENTS

For permission to reproduce copyright material the author and publishers gratefully acknowledge the following:

Cover (top and bottom) J.C. Revy, Science Photo Library
Page 4 (top left) The Hulton-Deutsch Collection (bottom) The Metropolitan Police Service **page 5** (middle) Frank Wiles, Mary Evans Picture Library (bottom) The Image Bank **page 6** (top) Martin Dohrn, Science Photo Library (bottom) The Metropolitan Police Service **page 7** (top) The Metropolitan Police Service (right) Mary Evans Picture Library **page 8** (top) Alfred Pasieka, The Image Bank (bottom) Foster & Freeman Ltd **page 9** Philippe Plailly, Science Photo Library **page 10** (top) JC Revy, Science Photo Library (bottom) Michael Gilbert, Science Photo Library **page 11** (top) Peter Menzel, Science Photo Library (bottom) James Holmes, Cellmark Diagnostics, Science Photo Library **page 12** (top) Sally Morgan, Ecoscene (bottom) RL Manuel, Oxford Scientific Films **page 13** (left) CNRI, Science Photo Library (right) Mary Evans Picture Library **page 14** (top) Horst Thanhaeuser, The Image Bank (bottom) Sally Morgan, Ecoscene **page 15** Foster & Freeman Ltd **page 16** Dr Jeremy Burgess, Science Photo Library **page 17** (top) Brown, Ecoscene (bottom) National Library of Medicine, Science Photo Library **page 19** (top left) Otto Rogge, NHPA (top right) Stephen Dalton, NHPA (middle left) Stephen Dalton, NHPA (middle right) Stephen Dalton, NHPA (bottom) L Campbell, NHPA

page 20 (top) Manfred Kage, Science Photo Library (bottom) Ronald Tom, Oxford Scientific Films **page 21** (top) Ronald Toms, Oxford Scientific Films (bottom) The Metropolitan Police Service **page 22** Adrienne Hart-Davis, Science Photo Library **page 23** Stephen Dalton, Oxford Scientific Films **page 24** (top) The Metropolitan Police Service (bottom) Sheila Terry, Science Photo Library **page 25** (right) Michel Tcherevkoff, The Image Bank (left) Dr Jeremy Burgess, Science Photo Library **page 26** (top) Jody Dole, The Image Bank (middle) Sally Morgan, Ecoscene **page 27** (top) Foster & Freeman Ltd **page 28** (top) Sheila Terry, Science Photo Library (bottom) Johannes Hofmann, Okapia, Oxford Scientific Films **page 29** Jerry Mason, Science Photo Library (bottom) E Hanumantha, NHPA **page 30** (middle) Geoff Tompkinson, Science Photo Library (bottom) Mary Evans Picture Library **page 32** The Metropolitan Police Service (bottom) Hicks Photographic Services **page 33** Hicks Photographic Services **page 34** (top) Sally Morgan, Ecoscene (bottom) Nicholas Foster, The Image Bank **page 35** (top) The Forensic Science Service (bottom) The Hulton-Deutsch Collection **page 36** The Metropolitan Police Service **page 37** (top) Labat/Lanceau, Jerrican, Science Photo Library (bottom) The Hulton-Deutsch Collection **page 38** (top) Michel Tcherevkoff, The Image Bank (bottom) The Metropolitan Police Service **page 39** Jerry Young **page 40** Jerry Young **page 41** Jerry Young **pages 42 and 43** The Metropolitan Police Service

CONTENTS

INTRODUCTION

A fingerprint expert at work in the 1940s. Today, modern technology has sped up the matching process.

A forensic scientist looks at a DNA fingerprint (see page 10).

Scientists believe that it is impossible for someone to commit a crime without leaving something behind or taking something away with them. If these traces of evidence can be found, they may provide the proof needed to bring the criminal to justice. They may take the form of fingerprints, hairs, fibers from clothing, tiny traces of chemicals, documents, bullets, or fragments of glass. This evidence is collected and studied by forensic scientists. Forensic means "applied to the law."

Science is applied to crime-fighting more now than ever before. As people find new ways to commit crimes and new ways to cover their tracks, scientists develop new techniques for linking suspects with their crimes and proving their guilt. Old techniques are constantly being improved so that they can be applied to smaller and smaller traces of materials. In the past, there was no way of identifying a criminal unless he or she was caught "red-handed" – that is, actually committing the crime. If the criminal got away unseen, there was no way of proving who had done the deed.

Nowadays the story is very different. Forensic scientists have an enormous variety of tests, techniques, and equipment that enable them to collect the tiniest pieces of evidence and identify them. The range of their work is so great that any one scientist could not possibly be expert in all of it. So, forensic scientists often specialize in one branch of their work. There are specialists in documents, firearms, fires, explosives, chemicals, poisons, and handwriting. Several specialists may be needed to collect all the evidence from the scene of a crime or from a suspect.

Other scientific specialists who are not full-time forensic scientists are often called in to help when their skills are needed. Psychologists can give the police a description of the type of person they are seeking. Insect specialists, called entomologists, advise on insects found during an inquiry, and so on. All of these scientists work together as a team to try to reveal the story of a crime that might otherwise remain secret. **Crime-fighting** looks at the work of forensic scientists and explains some of the methods they use.

A VICTORIAN DETECTIVE

When the investigation of crimes by the police was still in its infancy and before forensic scientists as we know them today existed, one famous figure was already able to solve crimes by "reading" clues left by the criminal. The ways in which he collected facts and worked out what they meant was very similar to the methods that police officers and forensic scientists use today. He was Sherlock Holmes. Many people still believe that Sherlock Holmes was a real person, but actually he never existed. He was invented by the author, Sir Arthur Conan Doyle. Doyle's stories about Holmes and his assistant

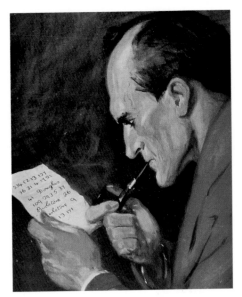

Sherlock Holmes

Dr. Watson first appeared in England in the *Strand* magazine in 1891, and they continued until 1925. Holmes lived at 221B Baker Street, London, a real address which is visited by people from all over the world.

Plays and films about the famous detective and the cases he solved are still popular today.

HISTORY SPOTLIGHT

History Spotlight boxes focus on an important technique, a piece of equipment, or a key figure in the history of some of the topics.

Modern forensic science can be traced back to the middle of the 19th century. By the 1850s, policemen were beginning to look for clues at the scene of a crime that might lead them to the person responsible. Scientists began to take an interest in the new field of criminology, too, and forensic science was born. The new science was pioneered in France, where the first forensic science laboratory was set up in 1910. The first American forensic science lab was set up in Los Angeles in 1923.

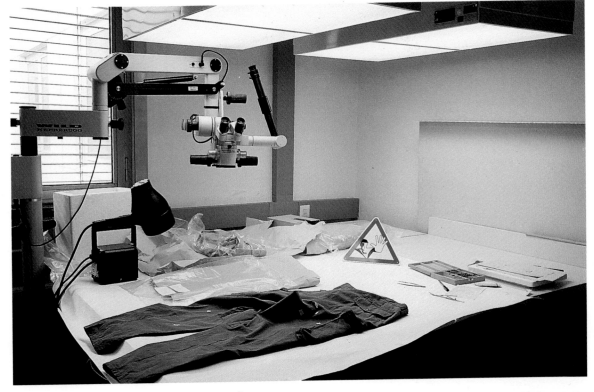

Pieces of evidence gathered from the scene of a crime.

FINGERPRINTS

Each person is a unique combination of hundreds of different factors – size, shape, eye color, hair color, skin color, and so on. Yet until 1900 there was no scientific way of using any of this information to identify someone. Crime-fighters needed one simple measurement or mark that would be unique to each individual. The fingerprint is just such a mark. It is not the only means of identification, but it has become the most widespread. It is used all over the world.

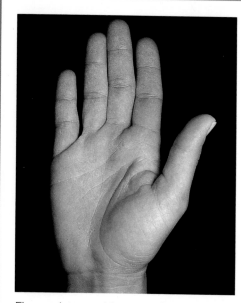

Fingerprints provide some of the best clues to a person's identity.

Fingerprints are normally invisible, so the first task at the scene of a crime is to find them. The invisible prints are called latent prints, and the process of making them visible is called developing. Forensic scientists normally develop latent prints by brushing a fine aluminum "dusting powder" over places where prints are most likely to be found – around doorknobs, drawers, window latches, and handrails, for example. The fine powder is trapped by the lines of sticky secretions left behind by the fingers. Black powder is used on pale surfaces to make the prints stand out more clearly. They can then be photographed. Fingerprints can even be taken away to the laboratory. They are removed by sticking a piece of clear adhesive tape over them. When the tape is peeled away again, the powder pattern of the print sticks to the tape. The tape can then be stuck onto a piece of cardboard and taken away for closer examination.

Dusting for fingerprints.

CLASSIFYING FINGERPRINTS

An identification system has to work quickly. It would obviously take far too long to compare fingerprints found at the scene of a crime with all the prints held on file. The Federal Bureau of Investigation (FBI), for example, has more than 80 million criminal fingerprint records, and millions of noncriminal records from people such as government employees. London's

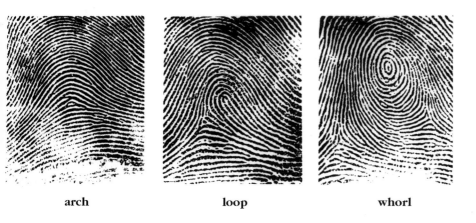

arch   **loop**   **whorl**

Most people (65 percent) have loop patterns on their fingertips. Three in ten have whorls, and the remaining five percent have arches.

An arch fingerprint with the points used to check a person's identity. The points may be where ridges come together, end, or divide in two.

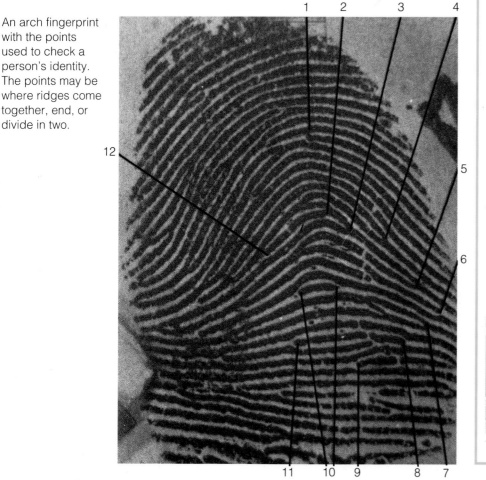

In the 1870s, photographs were used to keep records of criminals. But there was no way of classifying people or their photographs. A French police clerk, Alphonse Bertillon (1853-1914), tackled this problem by classifying people according to their measurements. When anyone was brought in for questioning by the Paris police, Bertillon took measurements from the suspect. To these he added two photographs and a description. The scientific name for the system is anthropometry, but it became known as the Bertillon system. When a suspect was arrested Bertillon took his measurements and compared them with those on file. If he found a match, the photographs and description would confirm the identification. But it was a very complicated system, and its success depended on the measurements being accurate to within a millimeter. By the 1890s, a much simpler and more reliable system called dactyloscopy (fingerprinting) was being developed. It replaced the Bertillon system in the early 1900s.

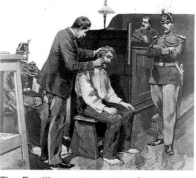

The Bertillon system at work.

Metropolitan Police has about four million fingerprint records in its computer files. Fortunately, fingerprints are classified (divided) into different types, according to their pattern. This reduces the search time.

The basic system was developed by Sir Edward Henry, the Inspector General of Police in Bengal, India, in 1900. It was so successful that it was adopted by police forces all over the world. According to the Henry classification system, all prints fall into one of three basic types – loops, whorls, and arches – named after the pattern of lines on the fingertip. Each of these groups is subdivided into smaller groups, according to differences in the pattern detail within each group – the arch pattern, for example, may be plain or "tented." There is also an "accidental" type made up of a combination of the three basic patterns. An unknown print found at the scene of a crime and a known print held on file are accepted by courts of law as coming from the same person if they are identical at a minimum of 12 points.

A computer image of a fingerprint.

MODERN FINGERPRINTING METHODS

Fingerprints have been used to help identify criminals for almost 100 years. In that time, many new scientific research methods have been developed. Some of them have provided scientists with new ways of finding and developing fingerprints.

This portable light source can be used in the laboratory or at the scene of the crime to show up fingerprints. The scientist wears goggles to protect her eyes from the very intense light.

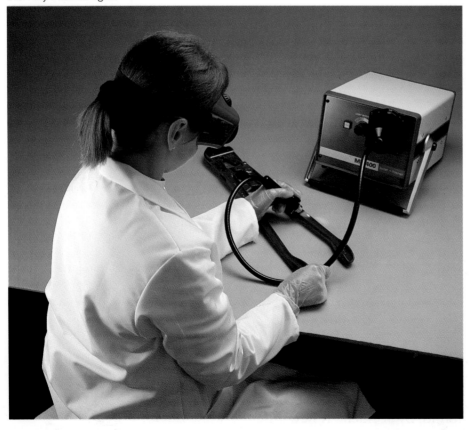

The traditional way of dusting surfaces for fingerprints is still used most of the time. In many cases it works well, but sometimes different methods are needed. Forensic scientists can now use a small portable laser to look for fingerprints. The scientist "paints" the scene of the crime with the laser beam. As the beam sweeps across doors, walls, and furniture, any fingerprints present on them glow, because they are fluorescent. Some molecules in the print absorb the laser light, and then release it again in the form of light of a different color. All of these tiny flashes combine to make the whole print glow when the laser beam hits it.

The technique of laser-sweeping enables large areas to be searched quickly, and prints in odd places can be found. Dusting the same surfaces with powder would take much longer, and prints in unlikely places could be missed altogether. Prints found on certain surfaces by a laser can also be dusted with a fluorescent powder to make them show up even more clearly, so they can be photographed.

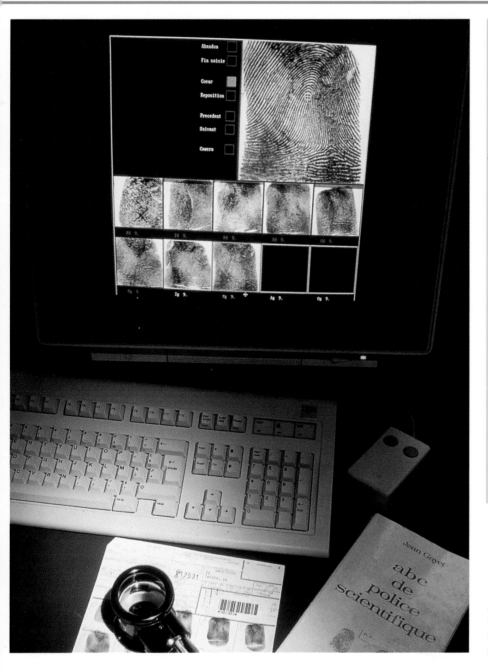

A "digitizer" (at the bottom of the picture), is used to convert old paper copies of criminals' fingerprint records into computer records.

PRINTS ON PAPER

It is difficult to detect prints on absorbent surfaces, such as paper, because the oil and sweat of the print sinks into the surface. Often these prints have to be developed chemically. A technique called fuming is sometimes used.

Fuming involves blowing chemical fumes over likely surfaces. The fumes react chemically with sweat or oils in any fingerprints, and they change color, revealing the print. Although the technique is old, new chemicals are still being tried to find the best one for developing clear images of prints. Iodine has been used as a fuming chemical for many years. Fingerprints turn yellow-brown when they are exposed to iodine vapor. But iodine is not the ideal chemical to use, because it is poisonous, and it does not always develop prints clearly.

In the early 1980s, another type of fuming chemical was found, by accident. A new type of glue popularly known as "superglue" had become available. Forensic scientists discovered that invisible fingerprints on an object turned white if the object was left near something that had been repaired with superglue. One of the chemicals in the vapor that is given off by the glue sticks to the print. As more and more glue vapor settles on the pattern of the fingerprint and hardens, the print itself becomes visible as a white mark.

GENETIC FINGERPRINTS

The human body is composed of billions of microscopic cells. Each cell contains a unique code, the genetic code that determines what we look like and how we develop. The code takes the form of long strings of molecules called DNA. No two people have identical DNA, unless they are identical twins.

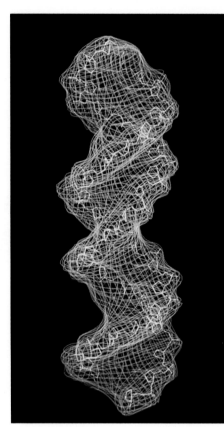

A computer image of a short section of DNA.

Techniques for getting the information of DNA were developed in the 1980s. DNA profiling, or genetic fingerprinting, was quickly taken up by the police and forensic scientists as a way of linking suspected criminals with their crimes.

MAKING GENETIC FINGERPRINTS

The process of making a DNA profile may begin with a scrap of stained clothing found at the scene of the crime. A tuft of hair or droplets of body fluids such as blood can be used, too. The material

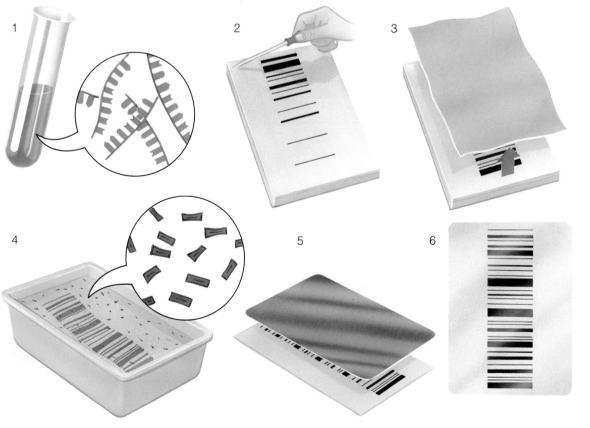

To make a genetic fingerprint, DNA is extracted from the body fluid (1), broken into fragments, and placed on a layer of gel (2). An electric current forces the fragments to separate into (invisible) bands, which are transferred to a nylon sheet (3). The sheet is placed in a bath, and short segments of radioactive DNA are added (4). Photographic film is laid on the sheet (5) and developed to reveal the "fingerprint" (6).

is soaked so that any body cells in the stain come away from the cloth and into the liquid. The cells are then broken open to let out the long threads of DNA. These are treated chemically to cut them into tiny pieces. A blob of these DNA fragments is then placed at one end of a layer of special gel.

When an electric current is passed through the gel from one end to the other, the pieces of DNA move through the gel in the direction of the electric current. The process is called electrophoresis. The shorter pieces of DNA can move through the gel more easily than the longer pieces. After a while, the DNA separates out into bands according to the size of the fragments, although at this stage the bands are invisible.

The pattern of DNA bands then has to be transferred to a nylon sheet. The nylon sheet is treated afterward with segments

A forensic scientist takes a blood sample from a stained pair of jeans. DNA from the sample will be used to provide a DNA fingerprint.

of radioactive DNA. When photographic film is laid on top of the nylon sheet for a while and then developed chemically, the bands of DNA appear as dark stripes on the film.

If the pattern of bands produced by cells found at the scene of the crime exactly matches the pattern made by cells collected from the suspect, then the body cells from both samples must belong to the suspect, and he or she must have been present at the scene of the crime. With a good sample that is rich in DNA, the chance of two people actually producing the same genetic fingerprint is only one in 2.7 million, which is good enough for a court of law. However, people who are related do have similarities in their DNA. The chance of two related people producing the same genetic fingerprint is as high as one in 200. If there is not enough good quality DNA material for a reliable test, the chance of two people producing the same genetic fingerprint could rise as high as one in 50. So, the value of DNA profiling depends entirely on the circumstances of the case.

A scientist compares DNA fingerprints on a lightbox.

TELLTALE TEETH

Fingerprints and DNA profiling ("genetic fingerprints") can often prove someone's identity beyond any reasonable doubt. But occasionally other methods have to be used. The mouth contains its own "print" that can identity its owner. Teeth and dental records are sometimes used to identify a criminal.

A bite mark on a piece of cheese.

No two people have exactly the same size and shape of teeth. However, teeth have never been used as a common identification system in the same way as fingerprints because, unlike fingerprints, "dental prints" can change. Over the years, teeth may become worn down or be lost due to disease and decay. Fillings and dentures would also alter a dental print. So the teeth of a person 20 years old would almost certainly look very different from the teeth of the same person at 60. Despite this, teeth can still often help to prove identity.

A hungry burglar who takes a mouthful of food at the scene of his or her crime may leave behind valuable evidence for the forensic scientist. When hard foods are bitten into, the remaining piece of the food retains a "print" of the teeth that bit into them. If photographs or casts of the teeth marks are compared to a suspect, a match between them can prove the burglar's guilt. The scientist must record the teeth marks quickly, because they will shrink and change shape if the food is allowed to dry out.

Teeth are also very useful for

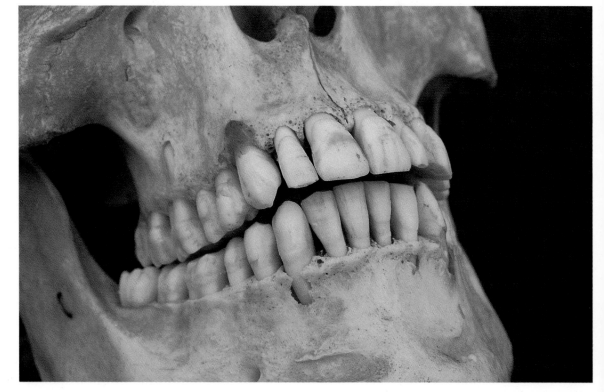

A full set of teeth in a human skull.

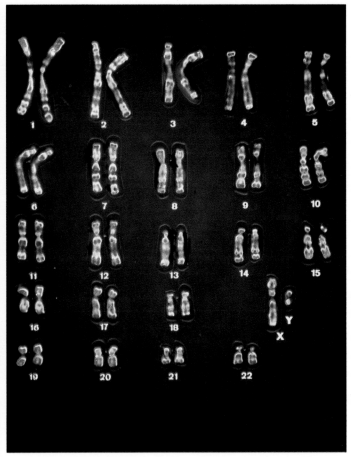

A computer image of pairs of chromosomes from a man. The nucleus of each human cell contains 23 pairs. Only men have Y chromosomes.

Dentistry of one sort or another has been carried out for over 2,000 years. A dental bridge made from gold was found in a Greek tomb dated to the third century B.C. It was tied to the owner's incisor teeth, so that it filled the gap between them. Painful teeth have been extracted for at least as long as this. Cavities in teeth were filled for the first time in the ninth century A.D. Dental drills were used in the Roman Empire from at least the first century A.D. They were operated by pulling a rope to make the drill spin. But the modern dental drill was developed in the United States in the middle of the 19th century. The first dental drills spun at about 600 revolutions per minute. The latest drills can reach speeds of almost half a million revolutions per minute.

A dentist's clinic in Paris in the 1890s.

identifying unknown bodies. If a body has lain undiscovered for a very long time, there may only be bones left, making identification all the more difficult. The size of the teeth can suggest whether the body is that of a man or a woman. Men generally have larger teeth than women. The state of the teeth – how much they are decayed or worn – can help in estimating the person's age. If any pulp (the material inside the tooth) is still present it can be stained with a fluorescent chemical that glows when a light is shone on it. The blobs of tissue that carry the cells' genetic code take up the chemical stain in a special way. The genetic code is contained in chromosomes, and it is only the Y chromosomes that become stained. Women do not have any Y chromosomes. So if any chromosomes glow when a light is shone on the stained tooth pulp, it proves that the tooth must have come from a man.

It may be possible to match dental work such as fillings or dentures with dental records of missing persons. If there is anything odd about the teeth, such as gaps or badly-shaped teeth, comparing a photograph of a missing person's smile in life to the teeth in the skull of an unknown body may be enough to prove the identity of the body. The branch of forensic science that deals with teeth is called forensic odontology.

DATA-DISKS ON TEETH

In the future, teeth may be even more useful as a means of identification. In 1986, American dentists began fixing a pinhead-sized disk to an upper molar of each patient. The tiny disk carries a 12-digit code that identifies the patient. If a body with one of these disks on a tooth is found, it can be identified easily by telephoning the dental register.

TOOLS AND TREADS

A footprint in wet sand.

W hen a burglar breaks into a building or a vehicle, he leaves marks behind on any windows or doors that he had to break or force open. If he drives over soft ground, the tires of his vehicle leave marks in the ground. And his shoes or boots may leave footprints in places. A lot can be learned from the marks a burglar leaves behind.

One screwdriver or chisel may look the same as many others, but each one gets knocked and scratched in different ways in its lifetime. The marks on its blade are almost as good as a fingerprint for identifying it later. If a tool-mark is found it is photographed. The forensic scientist then presses a pad of quick-setting plastic onto it. When the plastic sets and is peeled away, an impression of the mark is molded into the plastic. Tools found by the police can be compared with this. The tool used to make the mark will match the plastic cast exactly.

TIRE TREADS

When a vehicle is driven over soft ground, its tire tread patterns are pressed into the ground. The tread is designed to squeeze water out from beneath the tire, so that the tire grips the road in the rain. By examining the marks, a forensic scientist can tell in which direction the vehicle was traveling and whether it kept moving or stopped in one place for a while. Like tools, tires acquire unique marks. Cuts and embedded stones give each tire its own "fingerprint."

Like a fingerprint a tread mark can be photographed and lifted. When the tread pattern is photographed, the flashgun is held to one side so that the peaks and troughs cast shadows and show up the pattern more clearly. A ruler is laid alongside the print so that accurate measurements can be taken from the photograph. Lifting a tire tread print is not quite as easy as lifting a fingerprint. A "fence" of foil or cardboard is made around the tread pattern. Then quick-setting dental plaster is poured in. The ground may have been

A tire tread in damp soil.

A portable shoeprint lifter (below) that lifts indistinct dust marks of shoeprints. Lifting film is placed over the shoeprint and charged to attract the dust. The dust marks can then be removed and photographed in a studio. The lifter can lift prints from difficult surfaces, including paper and cardboard (right).

made water-resistant first, by spraying it with a fluid, such as shellac, to stop the plaster from soaking down into it. When the plaster has set hard, it provides a permanent record of the tire tread. Shoes often leave marks in soft ground in the same way as a tire tread. And the shoe print can be lifted in the same way, with plaster. Scientists can learn something about the suspect and his or her movements from footprints. Feet and shoes may also leave prints on smooth, polished floors. They are more difficult to see, but they can provide important clues about a suspect's size, weight, and movements.

Comparing two footprints under a powerful lens fitted with a bright fluorescent lamp.

HISTORY  SPOTLIGHT

Plaster casts of footprints were used to prove someone's guilt as long ago as 1786. Footprints were found in soft ground near the scene of a murder. Plaster casts of the prints were made and compared to the boots worn by a suspect. The casts and the boots matched exactly. The suspect was found guilty of the crime and executed.

SOIL, SEEDS, AND POLLEN

Nature is often a great help to the forensic scientist. The seeds of some plants are often found only in certain places and at certain times of the year. If they are carried away on the clothing of a suspect or the victim of a crime, they can provide valuable evidence.

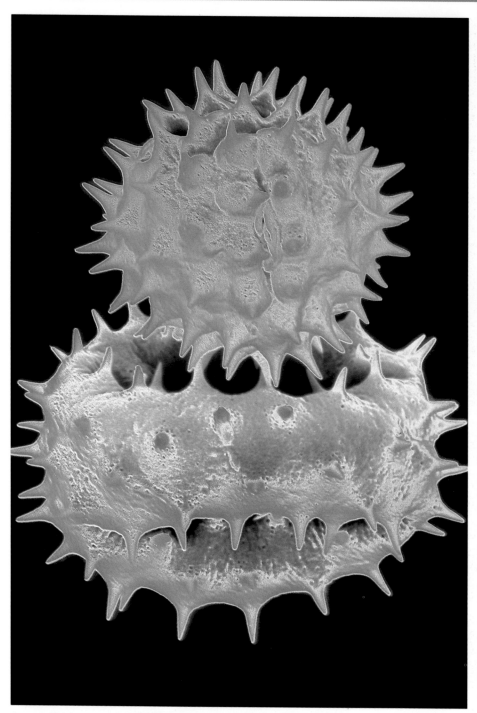

A magnified computer image of pollen grains from a marigold flower. The barbs may hook on to the body of an insect – or a person's clothes.

Pollen falling from the catkin of an alder tree.

Any criminal who walks over a field or garden, squeezes past a hedge, is knocked to the ground in a struggle, or goes anywhere near plants stands a good chance of picking up seeds, flower petals, pollen, or other pieces of vegetation on his or her clothes. And it may help to prove that a suspect could have been at or near the scene of a crime. If, for example, a house is robbed by someone who had to stand in a bed of roses to break a window, the presence of pollen from the roses in the suspect's clothes could link the suspect to a specific scene. If the plants are caught in the suspect's clothes, traces of fiber may be found clinging to them and the case against him or her is

All kinds of natural clues, most of them microscopic, could cling to a person walking in this field.

The use of natural clues in forensic science depends on the ability to classify plants and their seeds and pollen accurately. The principles that scientists use for naming and classifying plants (and animals) today were established by the Swedish botanist Carl von Linné (1707-78), who is better known by the Latin form of his name, Carolus Linnaeus. He gave each of the plants he knew a name with two parts – the system is therefore known as binomial nomenclature. The first name is the plant's genus, and the second is its species. Plants that are similar and which can breed easily with each other are placed in the same species, and species that share common features are placed in the same genus. For example, the primrose is of the Primula family, coming from the Latin word *primus*, meaning first, because the primrose usually blooms early in the spring. One species of primrose is known as *Primula denticulata*, meaning toothed leaved, while another is *Primula marginata*, because it has a silvery-white margin on the leaves.

strengthened even more.

Soil, too, can yield vital clues. If, for example, a footprint is found in soft earth outside a burglarized house, it may not show enough detail to prove conclusively that it was made by a similar shoe found in the house of a suspect. It may be an average size of a popular shoe that many people wear. However, if traces of the soil from the scene of the crime are found on the suspect's shoes or a tread from the sole is found on the ground that could be more difficult for the suspect to explain.

Soil is a rich mixture of chemicals, mineral grains of different sizes, plant material, and microscopic organisms. Some soils are acidic, others are alkaline, and many are neutral. They contain a wide range of different chemicals – chlorides, phosphates, carbonates, sulphates, and nitrates – in different proportions. A close match between the soil found on the shoe and soil at the scene of a crime cannot prove that the soil on the suspect's shoe must have come from the scene of the crime – other nearby fields and gardens probably have a similar soil type. But the match would add one more piece of evidence that the suspect has to explain. If natural clues like these may be of use, a forensic scientist will take the suspect's clothes to the laboratory and clean them by brushing, vacuuming, and using Scotch tape to remove particles. The scientist examines all the material collected under a microscope, and lists all the seeds and pollen present. By carrying out simple chemical tests on soil traces, the soil type can be added to the list. Even if the scientist has not visited the scene of the crime, he or she may be able to tell the police what types of plants are growing nearby and what sort of soil is present.

The Latin name for the white poppy – *Papaver somniferum* – is shown on this 19th-century drawing.

INSECT HELPERS

Detectives need to know when a person died to help them to work out what happened to him or her. Knowing the time of death accurately can eliminate some suspects and bring others under suspicion. Sometimes forensic scientists enlist the help of insects.

When any living creature dies, a series of natural changes takes place. The three most obvious changes that occur in human bodies in the hours immediately after death are known as algor mortis, livor mortis, and rigor mortis, which mean the temperature, color, and stiffness of death.

When someone dies, chemical activity ceases, and the body begins to cool down at the rate of about one degree per hour. So the temperature of a body can be used to estimate when someone died, provided that the surroundings in which the body is found are taken into account. A hot room or a chilly winter's day will alter the body's natural rate of cooling.

The color of a body is important. Blood is normally pumped around the body by the heart. When the heart stops, the blood sinks to the lowest part of the body. After a while, the red blood cells begin to break down and red hemoglobin leaks through the walls of the vessels into the surrounding tissues. The red color becomes fixed and is observed on the skin. If a body is moved some time after death, perhaps from lying on its left side to its right, this color change will not be at the lowest part of the body any more – a very suspicious circumstance.

The changes that occur after death also cause a stiffness in the muscles, which increases and spreads over the whole body in about 12 hours and then gradually goes away again. Rigor mortis is completely gone after about 36 hours. So any stiffness in the body helps to identify the time when death occurred.

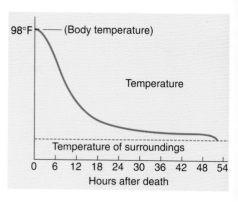

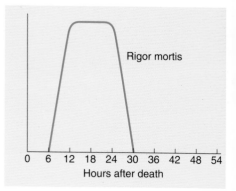

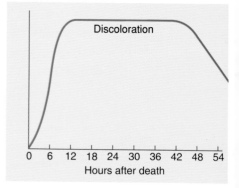

FLY CLOCKS

Flies can help the forensic scientists trying to estimate how long a body has lain undiscovered. When any living creature dies, organisms ranging from microscopic fungi and bacteria to worms and larger animals look upon it as a source of food. A human body is no different. It, too, falls prey to all of these organisms and animals. It may be an unpleasant thought, but it is a natural event, and as it

A bluebottle lays its eggs on a dead rat.

These bluebottle eggs will soon hatch into larvae.

Bluebottle larvae.

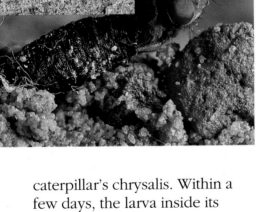

A bluebottle hatches out of its pupa case, only two or three weeks after the egg was laid.

There is a case on record of wasps helping to fix the time of someone's death. By the time the body was found, it was just a skeleton. It was obviously at least a year old, but how old? Five years? Ten years? Twenty years? Luckily for the scientists, a colony of wasps had set up home in the skull. From the state of the nest, entomologists could estimate the year in which the wasps had started building it. And the body must have been lying in the same spot for a year before that to reach a state that enabled the wasps to move in. This enabled the police to search the right year of their missing persons' records and to avoid wasting time searching through records for earlier and later years.

A wasp's nest in an attic.

happens it can be useful to forensic scientists.

Flies are particularly helpful. Some of them, such as bluebottles, seek out dead animals on which to lay their eggs. The eggs hatch within a day or two into tiny larvae, which feed on the body.

The fly larvae grow by molting – throwing off each skin as it becomes too small. Each stage is called an instar. Different species of flies go through different numbers of instars before the larvae change into a pupa. This is similar to a caterpillar's chrysalis. Within a few days, the larva inside its pupa case develops into an adult fly. The whole process from egg to adult takes two or three weeks. The stage the insects reach by the time a dead body is found enables insect specialists called entomologists to count back the days to when the eggs must have been laid. A body, whether it is a mouse or a man, does not lie for very long before flies discover it and lay their eggs. The unsuspecting insects act like a clock for the forensic scientist.

Diatoms, magnified many times.

Collecting a sample of river water for analysis.

WATER'S SECRETS

Clear water in a stream or the sea looks much the same as tap water, but it is not. Water taken from different places contains different chemicals and different living organisms. In other words, water carries its own "fingerprint." To forensic scientists, this watery fingerprint is very important.

If water is involved in a crime, a sample of the water is always taken for analysis. For example, when a body is found in water, it is important to find out if the person was still alive when he or she entered the water. If this is the case, then water will have been sucked into the lungs and transported by the blood to various parts of the body. Chemicals and microscopic organisms in the water are also carried around the body, and they can be detected by chemical analysis and also by looking at samples of body fluids under a microscope.

A group of organisms, called diatoms, is particularly important in any inquiry involving water analysis. The word diatom comes from a Greek word, *diatomos*, which means "cut in two." Diatoms are so-called because they are encased in a two-part shell. The types of diatoms found in water vary from place to place, depending on the properties of the water. The varieties of diatoms found in freshwater are different from those found in seawater. Diatoms found in the same type of water but in different places may also differ. The different varieties are easily identified by looking at the diatoms under a microscope, because each of them has a different shape of shell.

Scientists can analyze water in a number of other ways. They can test its salinity (saltiness), acidity, and hardness (the amount of salts such as calcium and magnesium bicarbonate dissolved in the water). Chemicals that may be found dissolved in water include the chlorine added to tap water to kill harmful organisms, and the fluoride added to help protect teeth from decay. If the water has come from a river or the ocean, it may contain particles of sand or soil. And if the water has come from a polluted area, it will also contain the chemicals that have polluted the water. Putting all these factors together may lead a forensic scientist to the spot where the water originally came from.

The sample of the water found around a body should be identical to any water found inside the body. This can be checked by identifying the chemicals and varieties of diatoms and other micro-organisms in the water. If they do not match, it suggests to

Filtering a water sample before testing for bacteria.

forensic scientists that the two water samples must have come from different places, and that the person did not die where the body was found. Then the question that must be asked is – how did the body come to be where it was found?

If no water at all is found inside the body, then the person must have died before he or she entered the water. The next questions the scientists have to answer are – how did the person die, and how did he or she then end up in the water?

HISTORY SPOTLIGHT

Many of the world's major rivers and commercial waterways have their own police forces. In Britain, the river police service is actually older than the police service on land. The Marine Police were established in Britain in 1798 to try to put an end to the high level of thefts from shipping on the Thames River through London. In 1839, the service became the Thames Division of the capital's newly formed Metropolitan Police. Police boats still patrol the Thames River today.

A police diver prepares to search the water.

HAIRS AND FIBERS

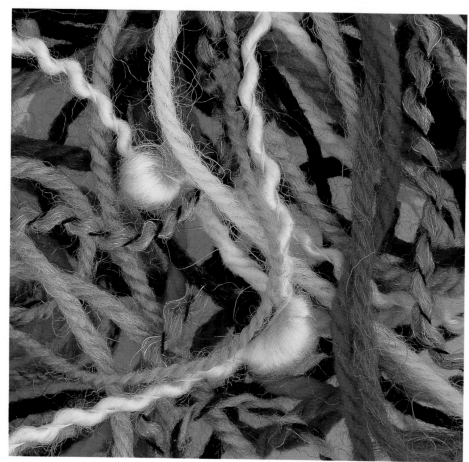

Woolen threads.

We are constantly dropping hair from our bodies and fibers from our clothes. It is difficult for a criminal and his or her victim to meet and touch without some hairs or fibers from one falling or rubbing off onto the other.

When the police close in on a suspect, his or her clothes, especially clothes that fit a witness's description of the criminal, are taken away for examination. Strips of clear tape are pressed all over them. Loose fibers stick to the tape, which is then examined under a microscope. Any fibers that do not belong to the clothes themselves may have been picked up from the scene of the crime, perhaps from the clothes worn by the victim or from carpets or curtains at the scene of the crime. By examining fibers collected from the victim of a crime or from property seized by the police, scientists may be able to tell the police what sort of material they may have come from. In one case, a drug dealer shed so many fibers from a rug into his illegal packages that forensic scientists who examined

the packages were able to describe the plaid pattern on the rug to police officers!

The fibers of different materials look quite different under a microscope. The first step is to try to match fibers from the scene of the crime with fibers found in the suspect's clothes or car. Any fibers that seem to have come from the same place can then be analyzed chemically to ensure that they really do match.

One method of analyzing fibers is called microspectro-photometry. With this process, white light is shone through the fibers. The dyes in the fibers absorb some wavelengths (colors) of light more than others. The light is then split into a spectrum of the separate colors that it contains by a component of the microspectrophotometer known as a monochromator. The intensities of the individual colors can then be measured by a second instrument, the components of the microspectrophotometer. Other types of this instrument can even measure invisible infrared radiation from the fibers. Different types of fibers produce different spectra.

Another method used for fiber analysis is thin-layer chromatography. It works by splitting up the colored dyes in artificial fibers into their separate parts. First, the dyes are extracted from the fibers. Spots of the solution containing the dyes are placed on a sheet of glass coated with silica gel and allowed to dry. The sheet is then stood up on end with one edge sitting in a small tank of solvent. The solvent rises up through the gel by capillary action, just as water rises up into a paper towel. When the solvent reaches the spots of dye, it keeps going, carrying the dye with it. Some dyes are made up of molecules that travel more rapidly than other molecules and so are carried farther. After a time, the dye has separated out into a series of colored bands. Each band contains a different chemical compound. If the fibers have been colored with a complicated mixture of dyes, the chromatography pattern on the glass can be very useful for matching fibers taken from a suspect with fibers collected from the scene of a crime.

It is not quite so easy to match hairs as it is fibers, because there are fewer types of hair than types of manufactured fibers. Even so, there are differences among individuals and it is quite easy to see the difference between animal hairs and human hairs, and between hair from the head and from other parts of the body, when they are examined under a microscope. By looking at the hair roots, it is also possible to tell whether the hair fell out or was pulled out. And there may be other features that make it possible for forensic scientists to match hair samples, such as color, and the use of bleaches and hair dyes.

Infrared Spectrophotometry

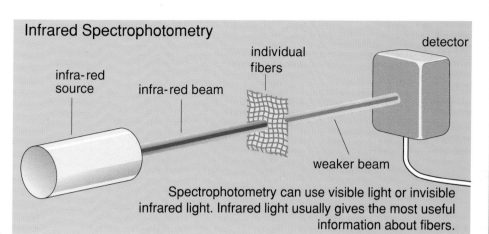

Spectrophotometry can use visible light or invisible infrared light. Infrared light usually gives the most useful information about fibers.

HISTORY SPOTLIGHT

The science of spectrum analysis, known as spectroscopy, was developed by the German scientists Robert Wilhelm Bunsen (1811-99) and Gustav Robert Kirchoff (1824-87) at the University of Heidelberg. The instrument they invented to analyze light, the spectroscope, was based on a prism (monochromator). A prism is a wedge-shaped block of glass that can split a light beam into its different colors.

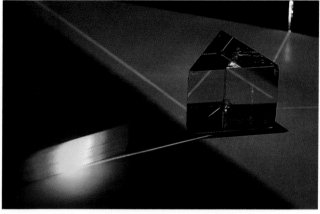

A beam of light divides into a spectrum of colors as it passes through a glass prism.

Thin-layer Chromatography

As the solvent rises up through the gel, the dye separates out into its different chemical compounds.

Bits
and
Pieces

When a crime is committed things often become broken. A window may be smashed to gain entry to a building. A car's paintwork may be scraped if it strikes something in the rush to get away. Forensic scientists are expert at finding the smallest fragments of material left behind after such events and analyzing them.

A forensic scientist collects evidence from a broken window.

Stress patterns in glass fragments.

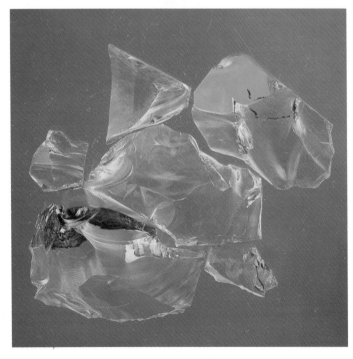

Glass is often broken during a crime. It may be a window, smashed to let a burglar into a building. It may be a soda bottle knocked over accidentally. It may be a car's headlight, broken when the car hit something. When glass shatters, the pieces can be sent flying over a wide area. And it is possible for the criminal to leave the scene with tiny slivers of glass caught in his or her clothes. If those pieces of glass can be found, it may be possible to match them with the broken glass found at the scene of the crime. If the broken window or bottle is reconstructed (stuck together again), the piece collected from the suspect may fit the glass jigsaw puzzle perfectly. As a double check, stress marks in the glass, called striations, which are caused by the intense heat used to manufacture the glass, should also exactly match from one piece to another.

The ability of glass to bend light, which is called its refractive index, varies from one type of glass to another. Forensic scientists measure and compare the refractive index of glass at the scene of the crime and any glass fragments found on a

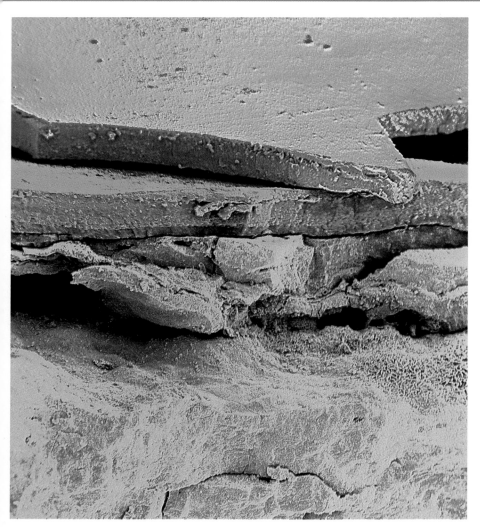

A magnified image of a flake of bodywork from a car, showing three paint colors. The yellow at the bottom is rust. (Image is enhanced by filters.)

HISTORY SPOTLIGHT

When a shopkeeper was killed by being hit with a bottle, a forensic scientist painstakingly reconstructed the bottle from the hundreds of glass fragments found nearby. Weeks later, a tiny sliver of glass was found by vacuuming furniture in the home of a suspect. It was a perfect fit in the reconstructed bottle. The glass proved something that the suspect's fingerprints, which were also found at the scene, could not prove – that the suspect had not just visited the scene of the crime earlier but was present when the crime was committed, because that is the only way that glass from the murder weapon could have been carried away by the suspect.

A scientist could reconstruct this panel of glass from the tiny fragments.

suspect's clothes to investigate whether they may have come from the same source.

Fragments of other materials can be carried away from a crime. When a car strikes something, or someone, tiny flakes of paint may be chipped off it. If paint flakes are found, the scientist can look at them edgeways under a microscope and see the different layers of paint in the flake. A repaired car can have a dozen layers of paint. The particular colors and order of the layers are different for different makes and models of cars. Scientists can look up this paint "fingerprint" in a computerized data base to find out the make, year, and of course color of car that the paint came from. If paint flakes found on an object or victim match paint taken from a damaged car, it is possible the suspect car may have struck the object or the victim. In the same way, flakes of paint or wallpaper scraped away as a burglar breaks into a building may stick to his or her clothes or to the tools that were used to force doors and windows open.

The pieces of material carried away from the scene of a crime by someone can be so small that they can only be seen clearly through a microscope. The scientist collects them by vacuuming the suspect's car or pressing Scotch tape all over the suspect's clothing. The contents of the vacuum cleaner bag and anything sticking to the tape are examined under a microscope for something that might have been picked up at the scene of the crime. The contents of the suspect's own vacuum cleaner bag are also frequently examined by scientists, in case the criminal has tried to remove evidence by vacuuming his or her home or car.

DOCUMENTS

Crimes often involve documents of one sort or another. A kidnapper may send a ransom note. A blackmailer may write to his or her victim. Entries in a diary may help to reveal a missing person's movements. Scribbled notes on a scrap of paper may hold vital clues.

Dollar bills being printed.

Entry and exit stamps in a passport.

There are several ways of examining documents to find out if they are genuine and have not been altered in any way. Documents fall into three broad categories – handwritten, typewritten, and printed. Handwritten notes and letters are most commonly involved in criminal cases. A questioned document examiner, a handwriting expert, may be able to tell whether a note is genuine from the way the letters are formed. Handwriting normally flows smoothly. Any sign that the writer has stopped and started or gone back over some letters to change their shape may indicate

that the note is actually a forgery.

Most of a written note may be genuine, but it may have been altered. Amounts on checks and dates on official documents may have been changed. If the police suspect that this may have happened, the ink on a document can be tested. Different inks respond to light differently. The document is lit by a series of lights, especially infrared and ultraviolet. Lasers may be used, too. Any alterations to a document will have been done in an ink that

matches the color of the original, but it is unlikely to match the original ink in every aspect of its chemical makeup. Different chemicals absorb and reflect different wavelengths (colors) of light in different ways. If a document has been altered, the alteration will show itself by glowing differently from the rest of the document under the test lights. Alterations to printed documents can be detected in the same way.

Typewritten documents can be almost as distinctive and individual as a sample of handwriting. In time, typewriter keys become worn, bent, and damaged. Faced with a typewritten note and a selection of typewriters taken from suspects' homes and offices, a document specialist will be able say which typewriter was used to produce the document. The paper on which a note is written or typed may be as useful as the message on it. Paper linked to a crime may be matched with paper found in a suspect's home. The torn edge of a ransom note may fit with a torn edge on a writing pad belonging to the suspect. A message may be made from letters torn out of a newspaper. A newspaper found in a suspect's home with appropriate pieces torn out could be difficult to explain!

Paper money bills are among the most valuable documents we have. It is important that they should be as difficult as possible to copy or forge. They are therefore often printed using special inks on special paper. The paper may have a watermark, a mark impressed on the paper when it is made and only visible when the paper is held up to the light.

The paper may also have a metal strip running through it. Different countries use different security measures, but all paper money has a very intricate design to make it as difficult as possible for anyone to copy.

This equipment allows scientists to detect document forgery. It reveals differences in dyes and pigments.

THE ESI EXAMINATION

When something is written on the top page of a pad, the next few sheets underneath carry an impression of whatever was written on the top sheet. And it stays there even when the original note has been torn off. A deep impression can sometimes be seen by shining a light across the pad at an angle, to throw the impression into shadow. Lighter impressions can be read by a special test called the ESI test – Electro-Static Imaging.

The test is performed by laying the marked sheet of paper over a wire mesh or metal sheet and covering it with a film of thin plastic. The wire mesh or metal sheet is charged up with electricity, and the charge is transferred to the paper and plastic film. When fine black powder is shaken over the plastic film, some of it sticks to the charged surface. It sticks more where there are any impressions in the surface and therefore reveals what was written on the sheet above it. If a note has been altered after it was

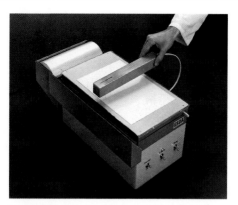

In the ESI test, the document is placed face up on the instrument and covered with a thin film. The film is then charged with electricity.

A fine powder is poured over the film until a clear image of the words appears.

written and torn off the pad, there will be differences between the document itself and the impressions revealed by the ESI test.

HISTORY SPOTLIGHT

In some cases, document analysis has come to the aid of people accused of crimes. In some recent cases involving people imprisoned for serious terrorist crimes, forensic document analysts were able to reevaluate the scientific evidence that was available at the time of the court cases. In particular, the ESI test was used to reexamine written records made by police officers of interviews with the accused people to see if their notes had been altered after the interviews.

ANALYZING BLOOD

If a burglar cuts his or her hand while breaking into a house, he or she will probably leave traces of blood at the scene of the crime. Forensic scientists are experts at analyzing blood and other body fluids to obtain important information about the person they came from

A blood sample.

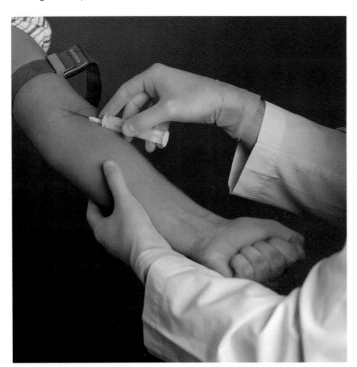

Taking a sample of blood from a vein.

A person's body fluids carry information that can help to identify him or her. All human blood is red and it all looks much the same, but there are several different blood types, or groups. They are not as unique to each of us as fingerprints, but they are still very useful to forensic scientists. If blood found at the scene of a crime is compared to blood taken from a suspect and they are the same type, then the suspect may be the person responsible for the crime. If the two blood samples are from different groups, then the suspect cannot be the person responsible for the crime. If the scene-of-crime blood sample and the suspect's blood sample are from the same group, further tests or a DNA profiling test (see page 10) may prove beyond reasonable doubt whether or not the two samples are from the same person.

BLOOD GROUPS

There are at least 14 systems for dividing blood into different groups. The first to be developed is called the ABO system. It is still used frequently in medicine but less so in crime detection. The ABO system divides blood into four groups. The groups are identified by analyzing molecules called antigens and antibodies. Red blood cells possess antigens and white blood cells release antibodies Different people have different kinds of antigens and antibodies, so they can be used to identify blood groups. Group O is the most common in the ABO system, followed by Group A. Type B is prevalent in Asia and Africa, but not as common among Europeans. Group AB is the rarest in the U.S. and Britain, and Type B is rare among Native Americans.

Another blood typing system is based on the fact that more than eight in ten people have one particular type of antigen on their red cells. People with this antigen are said to be rhesus positive. People who lack it are called rhesus negative. A rhesus test can be very important in medical science, but as so many of us are rhesus positive, a rhesus test is of little use in forensic science. Another more useful system is based on the fact that we all have proteins called enzymes and the form they take is determined by our genetic code. These "isoenzymes" exist in different forms in different people. So they can be very useful in narrowing down the identity of the person. The phosphoglucomutase group, called PGM for short, is one group of isoenzymes that is frequently used by forensic scientists.

If a blood sample found at the scene of a crime is shown to be Group O, the most common, and several other people who live or work at the scene of the crime also have Group O blood, the blood sample is of little value. But if the sample also contains a rare PGM isoenzyme, the scientist can then say that only one person among many could have left this particular trace of blood. If only one of the Group O people who live or work at the scene of the crime also has this relatively rare PGM factor, then that person would immediately come under suspicion.

When a trace of blood or other body fluid is found, it is dissolved in water and a spot of the solution is dripped onto a plate covered with gel. An electric voltage is applied across the gel. This makes the enzyme proteins in the sample move along the plate in the direction of the electric field. The process is called electrophoresis. Different enzymes travel different distances in the same time. After a time, the electric current is turned off, and the gel is treated chemically or illuminated by ultraviolet light to make the invisible enzymes show up as a pattern of bands. If the pattern produced by a suspect does not match the pattern produced from samples found at the scene of the crime, the suspect can be eliminated from the inquiry. Although many of these tests were originally developed to test blood, many of them will also work with other body fluids such as saliva.

Scientists testing blood samples.

HISTORY SPOTLIGHT

In 1900 the Austrian-born scientist, Karl Landsteiner (1868-1943) discovered the four major blood groups that are still used today. They were given their modern names – A, B, AB, and O – in 1910 by a Czech scientist, Jansky. In 1940, Landsteiner and two other scientists, Wiener and Levine, discovered another difference in blood types. It became known as the rhesus factor, because it was first seen by studying the blood of rhesus monkeys.

A rhesus macaque monkey.

CHEMICAL ANALYSIS

Forensic scientists are frequently called upon to analyze unknown substances found at the scene of a crime or in the course of a police inquiry. They may be substances that the police suspect to be poisons or drugs. There are now methods that can analyze and identify the tiniest traces of a chemical.

A scientist prepares samples to be tested in a mass spectrometer.

HISTORY SPOTLIGHT

Perhaps the most famous poisoning case was that of Dr. Hawley H. Crippen, who poisoned his wife, Belle, in 1910 and fled across the Atlantic with his mistress, Ethel Le Neve, on board the SS *Montrose*. His crime was discovered, and detectives were waiting to arrest Crippen on his arrival. Dr. Crippen was the first criminal to be caught by the use of wireless telegraphy.

Dr. Crippen and Miss Le Neve (center) are arrested.

Throughout most of recorded history, poison has been used by people who were impatient to inherit the wealth, property, or power of their superiors or older relatives. Personal advancement by poisoning was so common that poison became known as "inheritance powder." Kings, queens, and other high-ranking people in history feared the attentions of the poisoner so much that they often employed food tasters to check that meals were free from poison. Food tasting for an unpopular king could be a fattening but hazardous occupation! As "ordinary" people acquired more wealth during the 19th century, poisoning became even more widespread. The trials of poisoners were widely reported in the newspapers of Victorian times. Poisoning was common well into the 20th century.

People are rarely poisoned deliberately nowadays, because scientists have become so good at detecting all sorts of chemicals. Poisons work by interrupting or damaging the body's natural workings. Their effects may give away their presence, but sometimes chemical analysis is the only way of discovering them.

Scientists can identify an unknown chemical by splitting it up into a series of simpler compounds. One way this can be achieved is by using gas

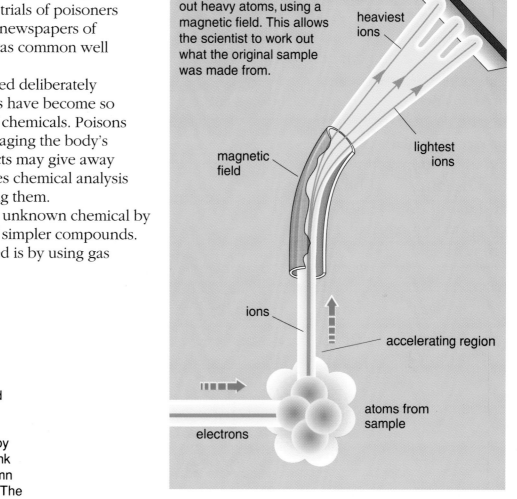

Inside a Mass Spectrometer

The mass spectrometer separates out heavy atoms, using a magnetic field. This allows the scientist to work out what the original sample was made from.

heaviest ions

lightest ions

magnetic field

ions

accelerating region

electrons

atoms from sample

Liquid Chromatography

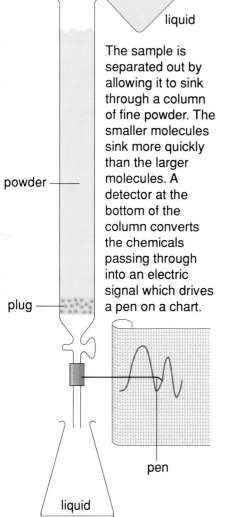

liquid

The sample is separated out by allowing it to sink through a column of fine powder. The smaller molecules sink more quickly than the larger molecules. A detector at the bottom of the column converts the chemicals passing through into an electric signal which drives a pen on a chart.

powder

plug

pen

liquid

chromatography, a more complex form of chromatography (see pages 22-23). This method uses a gas to separate components in a mixture instead of a solvent (see page 35). These simple compounds can then be split into even simpler fragments by placing them in the chamber of a mass spectrometer.

In the spectrometer, atoms from each chromatography band are bombarded by tiny particles called electrons. They give the atoms an electrical charge. These charged atoms, called ions, are sprayed into a magnetic field. This deflects the ions, or forces them off-course. The lighter ions

are deflected more easily than the heavier ions. The ions therefore become spread out and separated, with the lightest at one end and the heaviest at the other end. Detectors count the number of ions arriving and register where they come from. This tells scientists how many of which molecular fragments were present in the original sample. So, from this information scientists can tell which chemical compound was present in each chromatography band. And by putting all the results together from all the bands, the identity of the compounds in the original sample can be revealed.

FIREARMS

It is an unfortunate fact that more criminals carry firearms now than ever before. Fortunately, firearms specialists are expert at identifying the gun used to fire a bullet and can therefore link a weapon to a particular crime.

A policeman test-fires a gun.

Cartridges and bullets can provide clues. Notice the dent on the cartridge base (far left) and the rifling patterns on the two bullets (far right).

When a gun is fired, it leaves telltale marks on the bullet. All the bullets fired by the same gun are marked in the same way. If bullets found at the scene of one crime have identical markings to those produced by test-firing a weapon seized by the police, they must all have been fired by the same gun. Other clues can indicate how far the weapon was from a victim when the shot was fired, and the direction of the shot.

A cartridge holding the bullet has two parts. The front part of the major projectile or bullet is the metal pellet that is actually fired out of the gun. Behind that there is a charge of gunpowder called the propellant. When a gun's trigger is pulled, a spring-loaded hammer strikes the back end of the cartridge with great force, compressing (squeezing) and igniting a small charge called the primer in the cartridge's base. The primer in turn ignites the propellant. The energy released by the exploding propellant pushes the metal bullet out of the gun through the barrel.

The inside of a gun barrel has a series of grooves called rifling cut in a spiral from one end to the other. Different gun manufacturers use different rifling patterns. Rifling makes the bullet spin. Without rifling, the bullet could topple end over end, making it very inaccurate and reducing its range. A spinning bullet travels relatively straight through the air. The rifling cuts a unique pattern of marks into the bullet and identifies it forever as having been fired by one particular gun.

Cartridge cases, which hold a bullet until it is fired, are almost as useful as the bullet to a forensic scientist, because they carry the unique marks of the gun's ejector and the firing pin on the hammer. A revolver holds its full cartridges in chambers in a revolving cylinder. Every time the trigger is pulled, the cylinder turns so that a new cartridge is in front of the hammer. Spent (used) cartridge cases stay in the chambers until the gun is reloaded. Automatic weapons throw out each spent cartridge case when the gun is fired.

Shotguns have no rifling. The inside of the barrel is smooth, because the shotgun does not fire a bullet. It fires a package of tiny metal balls called shot. The chemical composition of the shot, the propellant, and fragments of material in the cartridge called wadding can tell scientists a great deal about the cartridge and the weapon that fired it. When a shotgun is reloaded, it ejects the empty cartridge cases, so, unless the criminal is incredibly neat, scientists will have the spent cases to examine.

The fully-loaded cylinder of a revolver.

HISTORY SPOTLIGHT

The first handguns were developed from small cannons in the Middle East in about the 13th century. The earliest recorded examples of police officers using the marks on bullets to solve a crime date back to the 1830s. In 1835, a Bow Street runner in London (the forerunners of the modern police) called Henry Goddard proved that a bullet said to have been fired by a burglar had in fact been fired by a butler at the house. This was because marks on the "burglar's" bullet exactly matched marks on bullets fired by the butler's own gun. Even before this, surgeons had sometimes noticed marks on lead balls fired by muskets. A bullet was first matched to a gun in the modern way, by comparing rifling marks on the bullet to rifling in the gun barrel, in 1889 in France. In that year, Professor Alexandre Lacassagne looked at a bullet taken from a murder victim and compared its markings with the rifling grooves cut into the barrel of a gun found nearby. The two matched, and the gun's owner was found guilty of murder.

FIRE

Fire, whether started by accident or deliberately, as in the crime of arson, can destroy evidence of another crime. Fire consumes documents, photographs, fingerprints, clothing, furniture, chemicals, and most other evidence. But some clues do survive fire.

A charred map.

The first thing a scientist may do on arriving at the scene of a fire is to sniff the air. Even though gasoline burns quickly and completely, the smell of gas or other flammable liquids used to start a fire may still hang in the air after the fire has been put out. Liquids like gasoline used in this way are called accelerants. If the

A fire that seems to have spread through a building more rapidly than normal is immediately suspicious.

Taking samples from the scene of a fire.

smell of the accelerant can be detected, then traces of the accelerant itself may be detectable in any absorbent materials like wallpaper, plaster, carpets, or woodwork. The forensic scientist will take samples of all of these for analysis later in the laboratory.

Chromatography (see pages 22 and 23) is used to split the accelerant into simpler chemical compounds that can be identified more easily. Unlike paper and thin-layer chromatography, which are used to analyze liquids, gas chromatography is used to detect and identify vapors. Vapor given off by a bag of remains from the fire is introduced into a flow of "inert" gas – a gas such as nitrogen, helium, or argon that carries the sample gas along but does not react chemically with it. The gas is pumped through a tube packed with a material (fibers or particles) that can absorb the vapor. The different gases present in the mixture are absorbed by the material at different rates, and therefore they appear at the other end of the column after different lengths of time. The different gases flow out of the column past a detector that drives a pen on a chart. As each compound appears, the pen registers its arrival by drawing a peak on the chart. Each type of accelerant is composed of a characteristic "cocktail" of compounds that produce an identifiable chart recording.

HISTORY SPOTLIGHT

In America, there was no attempt to set up an organization to control fires until 1648. Instead, rows of colonists formed "bucket brigades." One row would pass along buckets filled with water to throw on the fire; another row would pass back the empty buckets to the water source to be refilled. However, in 1648, in what is now New York City, the governor of the colony, Peter Stuyvesant, founded an organization to inspect for potential sources of fire. Later he arranged a patrol and alarm system to detect actual fires. Boston had the first professional fire brigade in 1679. Its equipment consisted of a hand pump to drench the fire with water. It wasn't until 1736 that America had its first volunteer fire department. It was established in Philadelphia by Benjamin Franklin.

Benjamin Franklin and his Union Fire Company, Philadelphia.

EXPLOSIVES

When a scientist is called to the scene of an explosion, it may not be clear whether or not a crime has been committed. The explosion may have been caused accidentally by a gas leak. The scientist's job is to find out what caused it. Forensic scientists are expert at reading the signs left by different types of explosive materials.

The site of a terrorist bomb blast.

A remote-controlled robot is used by bomb disposal teams to handle suspect items.

The effect of a blast itself gives the scientist the first clues as to what caused it. A gas blast causes a general pushing effect all around the seat of the explosion. Energy is released throughout the whole cloud almost simultaneously. A bomb blast travels out with immense force from a single point, but it dies away as it goes. The scientist can often tell the type of explosion by the pattern of devastation. Other clues come from tiny fragments of debris that have been flung into the walls and furniture near the seat of the explosion and become buried in them. By measuring how deep they are buried, the scientist can work out how fast they were flying. If the fragments were traveling at a speed of 3,000 feet per second or more, then a bomb is the most likely cause of the explosion.

If the scientist decides that the explosion has been caused by a bomb, the debris is sifted to look for pieces of the bomb. Tons of material may be taken away for careful examination in the laboratory. Even the tiniest pinhead-sized fragment can give a clue as to how the bomb was made and detonated. A fragment of printed circuit board may indicate that an electronic timer was used. Pieces of a watch or clock suggest a clockwork timer. An electronic timer could have been set months before, whereas a clockwork timer is only effective over a time delay of several hours at most. This helps the police to narrow down the time period when the bomb was planted and enables them to search for witnesses who might have been nearby at that particular time.

How do scientists know whether a part of a watch, for example, has come from the bomb and was not an "innocent" watch unconnected with the bomb? The high temperature flash at the heart of a bomb explosion leaves its mark on the materials closest to the detonation. Scientists look out for this characteristic burning or melting on suspicious items.

HISTORY SPOTLIGHT

The modern history of explosives began with a Swedish chemist called Alfred Bernhard Nobel (1833-1896). Two explosives called nitrocellulose and nitroglycerin discovered in the 1840s were very powerful but also very dangerous to make and use because they were unstable – they could explode at any moment, particularly if they were handled roughly. In 1867, Nobel discovered that an explosive that was easier to control could be made by soaking liquid nitroglycerin into a fine powder called *kieselguhr*. This is a natural powder produced by the microscopic skeletons of millions upon millions of prehistoric sea creatures called diatoms. Because of this, it is also called diatomaceous earth. Nobel called his new explosive, dynamite. He used the vast fortune he amassed from his discovery of dynamite to establish the Nobel Prizes that are still awarded today for achievements in physics, chemistry, physiology or medicine, literature, and peace. An extra award for economics was added in 1969.

Alfred Nobel

MAKING PICTURES

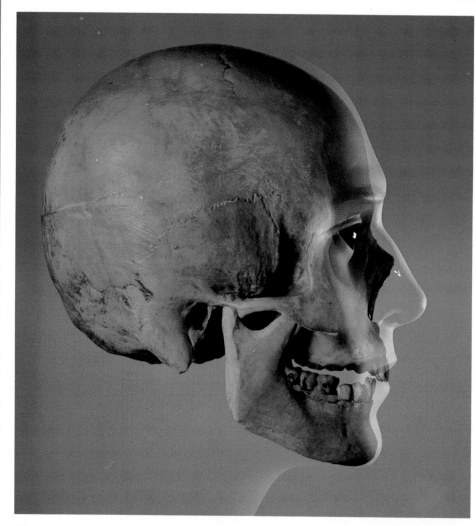

A computer image of a face built up on a human skull. Such images can help to identify bodies.

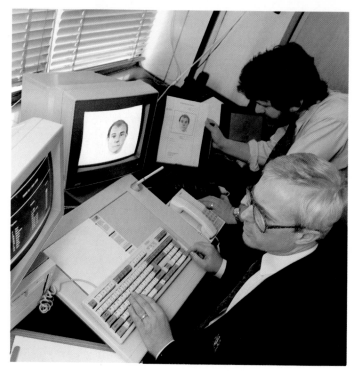

Photofit pictures can help to track down suspects.

Someone who sees a person committing a crime may have a clear picture of the criminal in his or her head. The police can only make use of what the witness has seen by turning that mental picture into something that everyone can see – a picture of the suspect.

In the past 50 years or so, the police have used several systems for creating a picture of a suspect. One of the first, called Identikit, was developed by Hugh McDonald in the United States and introduced by the Federal Bureau of Investigation (FBI) here in the 1950s. It was used by selecting drawings of facial features from a kit containing hundreds of drawings of noses, chins, mouths, ears, eyes, hairlines, and other facial features. The separate features were put together in a frame to form a face. The Identikit officer worked alongside the witness. If the witness felt that the nose in the picture was too broad or the eyebrows too thick, the officer could change them until the witness was satisfied that the face resembled that of the suspect.

The major drawback of the Identikit system was that the picture it produced wasn't

A scientist prepares to build a model of a face based on the cast of a skull.

The technique of plastic or facial reconstruction was developed by a Russian professor called Mikhail Gerasimov from earlier work pioneered at the end of the 19th century in Switzerland. Gerasimov was an archaeologist and anthropologist. He studied our ancestors, the people who lived in prehistoric times. He used facial reconstruction to produce lifelike models of how prehistoric people may have looked when they were alive. His work came to the attention of forensic scientists in Moscow, who wondered if the technique was accurate enough to reconstruct the appearance of more recent unidentified bodies. Gerasimov was asked to reconstruct no less than 12 skulls whose appearance in life was known to the forensic scientists but not to Gerasimov. Each skull was given a number to identify it. Gerasimov had no information about its "owner's" age, sex, color, or nationality. The experiment was an overwhelming success. All 12 skulls could be identified by comparing Gerasimov's reconstructions with photographs of the heads. As a result, the technique of facial reconstruction was adopted by Russian forensic scientists and Gerasimov became the first director of Russia's Laboratory for Plastic Reconstruction.

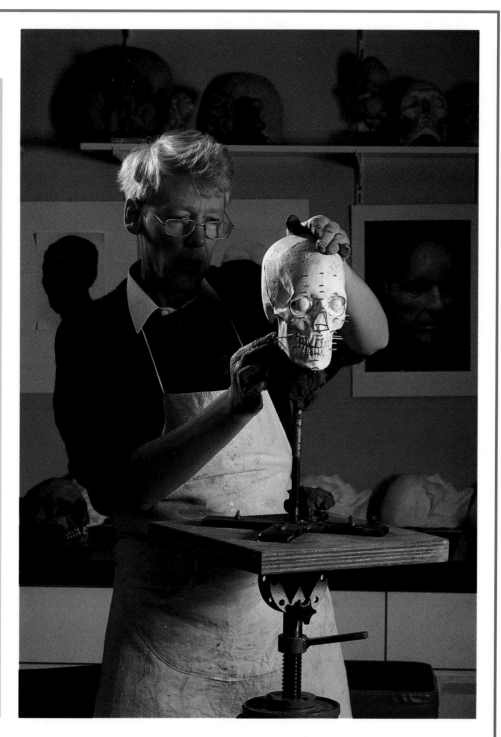

very lifelike. The Photofit system, devised by Jacques Penry in Britain in 1971, produces a more realistic picture than Identikit, because it builds up a picture of the suspect's face from photographs of parts of the face instead of drawings. Sometimes the best result can be obtained by a skilled artist working with the witness. Guided by the witness, the artist makes a lifelike drawing of the suspect. The latest techniques rely on computer images to build up a facial picture.

REBUILDING FACES

Identikit and Photofit, and modern techniques such as Video-fit and E-fit, all try to produce a picture of a living person from a witness's description. Occasionally, the

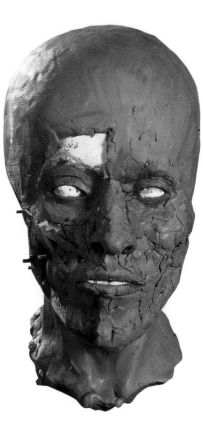

These pictures show some of the stages of reconstruction of an unknown victim's head.

police may have a rather different problem. They may have the difficult task of identifying a person from badly decomposed or burned remains. Dental records can sometimes help (see page 12). If the police have some idea of who the remains may belong to, they may superimpose a photograph of the skull on a photograph of the living person to see if they match. But if the police have no clues as to the person's identity, a special technique called facial reconstruction or plastic reconstruction is used to recreate the appearance of the living person in the hope that someone will recognize him or her.

The bones of our skull are covered by muscles and skin. Scientists know about where the muscles are and how thick they are at each point on a living person's face. They can use this knowledge to reconstruct a dead person's face. They make a plaster cast of the skull of the dead person, and insert wooden pegs into the plaster so that they stick out by the thickness of the flesh at that point on a living

person's head. The layers of muscle and skin are then built up in clay until the pegs are just covered. With false eyes, teeth, and hair, and realistic skin coloring, the result can be extremely lifelike. The reconstructed head is photographed and shown to people or published in newspapers. It has been successful in identifying people on many occasions.

MIND HUNTERS

When police officers are investigating a serious crime, they often form a mental picture of the person they believe is responsible. Their mental image is a combination of all the facts that are known about the person – age, height, weight, coloring, style of clothes, type of vehicle, and so on. In recent times a new and powerful factor has added even more detail to this image. It is called a psychological

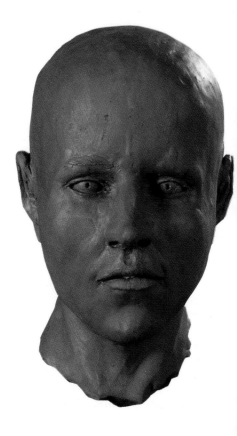

profile. The modern technique of psychological profiling was developed by the American psychiatrist, Dr. James Brussel. He was so successful in accurately predicting the type of person the police were looking for in a number of cases that the Federal Bureau of Investigation set up a psychological profiling unit in the early 1980s. By 1986, the British police, among others, were using psychological profiling, too.

An experienced profiler looks at the same scene of a crime as police officers and forensic scientists, but sees a different picture. While the police and scientists are looking for prints, hairs, fibers, fluids, and other physical evidence, the profiler sees signs of the criminal's feelings, such as anger or frustration, and patterns in the ways in which the criminal has behaved. The psychologist compiles an outline, or psychological profile, of the criminal. The profile may be very detailed, including even the sort of job the person may have and the style of clothes he or she is likely to wear. The profile enables the police to identify the most likely suspects. If psychologists can provide the police with a sufficiently detailed profile, there may be only one person that the police have interviewed who fits the profile in every respect. A computer can pick him or her out of its memory in seconds (see pages 42 and 43).

HISTORY SPOTLIGHT

The first person to develop ways of analyzing a person's personality was the Austrian psychiatrist Sigmund Freud (1856-1939). He showed how someone's early experiences, memories, feelings, and family relationships might affect their personality and behavior. One of the methods that Freud used to reveal the reasons why people behave in certain ways and what the causes of nervous illnesses might be was to analyze their dreams. This and other techniques that he developed became known as psychoanalysis.

USING COMPUTERS

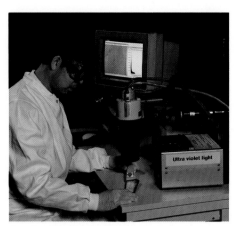

A scientist uses a computer to look at fingerprints on a knife.

Solving a crime is a process of collecting and sorting information and using it to identify the criminal. The computer's ability to process large amounts of information very quickly has made it an increasingly important aid in the modern business of crime-fighting.

Computers can do more than merely store information and find it again quickly. They can be programmed to process or analyze the information held in their electronic memory. This ability has sped up fingerprint identification. Before the computer age, fingerprints found at the scene of a crime had to be identified by someone comparing the unknown prints to each set of prints already held on file. One crime in 1961 resulted in six fingerprint officers spending six months comparing a print found at the scene of the murder with prints held on file. Nowadays fingerprint identification can be done much more quickly by computer, with a skilled fingerprint specialist making the final confirmation.

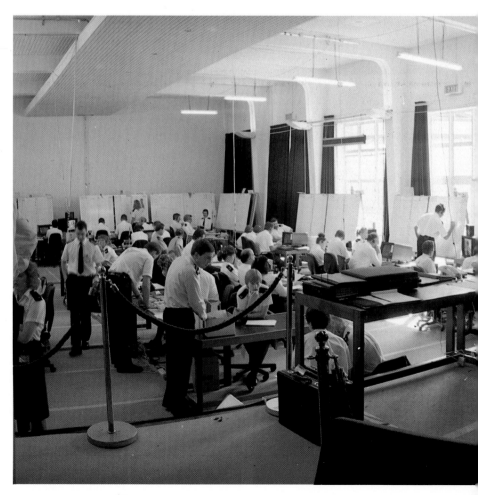

Computers play a key role in handling information received at the headquarters set up to investigate a serious crime.

A major police inquiry into a serious crime is an enormously complicated operation. The statements taken from witnesses and many other people who are indirectly linked with the crime may contain thousands upon thousands of individual pieces of information. All the clues necessary to solve the crime and identify the criminal may be buried in these statements, but it is very difficult and time-consuming to sift through the irrelevant information to find the few useful facts. However, computers can analyze information very quickly. For example, the police may believe that the person responsible for a crime may have lived or worked in a certain part of a town. They may feel that he or she might have access to printing equipment and is also a sports fan. The computer can search through every statement in its memory and find all the references to the people who satisfy these factors.

In many professions and industries automation is feared as a way of replacing people with machines. But computers will never replace the police officer and the forensic scientist, because computers can only do what they are programmed to do. Their value is that they can do very simple things extremely quickly. The inventiveness and versatility of the police officer and the forensic scientist will always be needed to develop and prove new theories and techniques. Computers and computer-controlled equipment are merely tools that supply vital information quickly to police officers and leave scientists free

HISTORY SPOTLIGHT

The first computers built during the 1940s were massive machines with up to 1,500 glass "vacuum tubes" or valves weighing several tons. They were extremely unreliable and needed a team of highly trained people to keep them running and to interpret their results. And the computers had to be rewired for each new problem they tackled. Computers like these were far too slow, cumbersome, and unreliable to be of any practical help to police officers and forensic scientists. It was the development of small, fast, and powerful computers in the 1970s that enabled the power of the computer to be brought to bear on the information storage and processing problems of crime-fighting.

to advance their work more rapidly than ever.

GLOSSARY

ABO system a method of dividing human blood into groups for purposes of identification in both medicine and crime detection.

Anthropometry a system for identifying people by measurements taken from their body.

Arson a crime involving the deliberate burning of property, such as a building.

Chromatography a scientific technique for separating a chemical compound into its simpler constituents by passing it through or over a material that slows down the progress of different substances at different rates.

Dactyloscopy another name for fingerprinting. A system for identifying people by their fingerprints.

Digitizer a system for converting an image, such as a fingerprint or a photograph of a person, into a code that a computer can store and process.

DNA DeoxyriboNucleic Acid. Long threadlike molecules in the cells of living organisms that control the growth and development of the organism. The genetic code.

Electrophoresis the use of an electric field to make particles move through a liquid.

Electrostatic electric energy based on the forces between electric charges.

Enzymes protein molecules that stimulate chemical reactions in the body – the chemical processes necessary to digest food for example.

Forensic scientists those scientists whose specialty is relating medical information to legal problems.

Fuming a process by which fingerprints, otherwise invisible, can be developed on a variety of surfaces by blowing certain chemicals over the surfaces.

Questioned document examiner person who studies handwriting.

Inert gas a gas such as nitrogen used in chromatography to move the sample to be identified through the equipment without reacting chemically with it.

Infrared invisible electromagnetic radiation beyond the red end of the visible spectrum.

Mass spectrometry a scientific technique for separating and identifying atoms and molecules according to their mass.

Refractive index the power of a transparent material such as glass to bend light. Useful for matching a piece of glass to glass from the scene of a crime.

Rifling the pattern of grooves found inside a gun barrel, which allow a bullet to be identified as having been fired from a specific gun.

Ultraviolet invisible electromagnetic radiation just beyond the blue-violet end of the visible spectrum.

Vapor the gaseous form of a substance that normally exists as a liquid or solid – water vapor, for example.

FURTHER READING

Ahouse, Jeremy J. *Fingerprinting.* Lawrence Science, 1987

Barber, Jacqueline. *Crime Lab Chemistry.* Lawrence Science, 1989

Billings, Charlene W. *Lasers: The New Technology of Light.* Facts on File, 1992

Bycznski, Lynn. *Genetics: Nature's Blueprints.* Lucent Books, 1991

Cohen, Sharron. *Mysteries of Research.* Alleyside Press, 1992

Dolan, Edward. *The Police in American Society.* Franklin Watts, 1988

Fine, John C. *Racket Squad.* Macmillan, 1993

Gardner, Robert. *Crime Lab. 101: Experimenting with Crime Detection.* Walker, 1992

Hill, John. *Exploring Information Technology.* Raintree Steck-Vaughn, 1992

Hooper, Tony. *Genetics.* Raintree Steck-Vaughn, 1993

Kusinitz, Marc. *Poisons and Toxins.* Chelsea House, 1992

LeVert, Marianne. *Crime in America.* Facts on File, 1991

Newton, David E. *Gun Control: An Issue for the Nineties.* Enslow, 1992

Steele, Philip. *Kidnapping.* Macmillan, 1992

Strahinich, Helen. *Guns in America.* Walker, 1992

Tesar, Jenny. *Scientific Crime Investigation.* Franklin Watts, 1991

Wormser, Richard. *Allan Pinkerton: America's First Private Eye.* Walker, 1990

INDEX

*Index numerals appearing in **boldface** indicate caption references.*